AF408657

Follow Your Creative Spirit

Bring Your Art to Life

by

Julianne Davidow

CAERUS PUBLICATIONS
NEW YORK
2024

Copyright © 2024 Julianne Davidow

All rights reserved. No part of this book may be reproduced, scanned, or distributed in any printed or electronic form without the written permission of the author, except for brief quotations embodied in articles, reviews, or used for scholarly purposes.

While every precaution has been taken in the preparation of this book, the publisher assumes no responsibility for errors or omissions, or for damages resulting from the use of the information contained herein.

If any required acknowledgements have been omitted, it is unintentional. If notified, the publisher will be pleased to rectify any omission in future editions.

FOLLOW YOUR CREATIVE SPIRIT: BRING YOUR ART TO LIFE
First edition: June 2024

ISBN: 979-8-218-38563-7 (e-book)
ISBN: 979-8-218-38564-4 (paperback)

Library of Congress Control Number: 2024905456

Cover design by Julianne Davidow
Photograph of *Due Angeli Musicanti*, detail, att. to Pier Maria Pennacchi, Church of San Pietro Martire, Murano

Caerus Publications
Your Creative Spirit, LLC
418 Broadway Suite N, Albany, NY 12207
www.juliannedavidow.com

Caerus Publications is an imprint of Your Creative Spirit, LLC

To my fellow creators; we are all creators.

Contents

This may sound too simple but is great in consequence. Until one is committed, there is hesitancy, the chance to draw back, always ineffectiveness. Concerning all acts of initiative (and creation), there is one elementary truth, the ignorance of which kills countless ideas and splendid plans: that the moment one definitely commits oneself, then Providence moves too. All sorts of things occur to help one that would never otherwise have occurred. A whole stream of events issues from the decision, raising in one's favour all manner of unforeseen incidents and meetings and material assistance, which no man could have dreamt would have come his way.—W.H. Murrary

Introduction

Practicing an art, no matter how well or badly, is a way to make your soul grow...—Kurt Vonnegut[1]

Do you yearn to create something of meaning and value that is uniquely yours? It doesn't matter how old or young you are or your life circumstances. You just know that something calls you to create. The creative call comes in various ways and differs from person to person. It may come in the form of an inner voice, an urge, a longing, a deep wish, a persistent fear, a recurring dream theme, or an image.

But along with the call to create comes obstacles. These obstacles are as unique as each person. Perhaps you are already working on a project but find it hard to work steadily, to fit your creative work into your schedule. Many well-known artists and entrepreneurs have faced enormous struggles and limitations. The Victorian writer Anthony Trollope (1815-1882) worked in the postal service for 23 years while writing novel after novel, rising at five in the morning to write for three hours a day. Franz Kafka (1883-1924) also worked in an insurance company and wrote late at night. James Baldwin (1924-1987) suffered from poverty and racism, worked many menial jobs, and attempted suicide numerous times, yet he continued to live, write, and become a lauded author.

Another obstacle may be that you're not sure what art form most calls to you. But nothing is stopping you from trying various media. Leonardo da Vinci (1452-1519) was a painter, engineer, scientist, visual artist, writer, and inventor; Michelangelo (1475-1564) was a sculptor, painter, and writer. William Blake (1757-1827) created an entire world of his own with both word and image. The psychologist C.G. Jung (1875-1961) was also a writer, painter, and sculptor; Anton Chekhov (1860-1904), famous for his plays and stories, was also a doctor.

Then, there is the obstacle of committing to do your creative work. You may think, "I'm not a great artist. I'll never be a Leonardo or a Blake." It may seem futile to begin—or continue—when the outcome is uncertain, and there are many other things to do. In addition, the world is such a troubled place. Isn't there a better use of time? But as many objections as you raise, you still feel that yearning.

This yearning to create can be joyful when you can channel and express it. It comes from a place of mystery and depth. You may not know where it begins or always know where it will take you, yet you feel compelled to follow it. And when you do, you can achieve what feels like a state of unity, of pure focus, even for brief periods. The process of creating something meaningful is an intimate act of communion. When you follow your creative spirit, you become a co-creator with nature, the spirit of nature that brought you into being.

The word spirit comes from the Latin *spiritus,* meaning breath. Our breath keeps us alive, but in its more profound sense, *spiritus* or Spirit is what inspires us and moves us to do what is important to us. A person's spirit is their very life force, which bestows life, energy, power, enthusiasm, and will. Following your creative spirit means developing trust in your talent and acting on those urges to bring the images, words, sounds, or feelings you carry inside out into the world. When you do this, no matter the outcome, whether you become 'successful' or not, you become more unified, and the other activities you engage in become more creative and fulfilling.

I've always found myself engaged in one creative activity or another. As a child, I made up dances, talked to myself in strange languages, appeared in school plays, studied ballet and piano, and wrote poems and stories. I studied painting, acting, photography, and writing as I grew older. Now, writing is my focus. I am always working on a book, story, or essay. Sometimes, I feel like one of those little green plants that grows through the cracks of a sidewalk. No matter what obstacles I face, I always manage to scribble something on a piece of paper.

I've also always been a spiritual seeker. Although I grew up in the Jewish tradition, I received little formal training. But even as a child I believed that there was some kind of unseen force or higher power that lay behind or within all of life. I was fortunate because in our house, we had a lot of books, and in our library, I found writings on the world's great religious traditions. When I discovered a quote from the Hindu *Bhagavad Gita*, I knew that there was a purpose to my life and that the words were key to something greater: "Never was there a time when I did not exist, nor you, or these kings; nor will there come a time when we ease to be."[2] This early discovery watered the seeds of my lifelong interest in philosophy and religion.

I have never abandoned the two paths I first walked as a child, the spiritual and the creative. For me, they overlap and are of the same essence. Both allow me to touch something that feels ephemeral yet very real. As writer and theologian Matthew Fox says, "Creativity is not a noun or a verb—it is a place, a space, a gather, a union, a where—wherein the Divine powers of creativity and the human power of imagination join forces..."[3]

When I read Thomas Moore's *Care of the Soul* and James Hillman's *The Soul's Code*, I learned about the Greek concept of the *daimon*, and it explained the desire I've always had to keep on creating, whether others understood or not. Later, when I started researching my book *Outer Beauty, Inner Joy: Contemplating the Soul of the Renaissance*, I delved deeper, exploring how Renaissance philosophers adopted the Greek idea that everyone is born with a creative spirit, the *daimon*, that accompanies us throughout life. *[In this book, I will use the spelling 'daimon' except when using direct quote].* The word *daimon* can be defined in several ways, such as a guardian angel, soul, inner twin, life companion, or heart's calling. Some people call it a higher self. Ancient philosophers said that each person has a particular task or tasks in this lifetime that the *daimon* helps us to fulfill.

Greek philosopher Aristotle used the term *eudaimonia,* meaning the highest good a person can experience. *Eudaimonia* consists of *eu,* the Greek word for good, and *daimon,* spirit. So, happiness or human flourishing comes from having a good relationship with our *daimon,* our indwelling creative spirit.

When we listen to the messages from our *daimon* and act on this source of inspiration, we flourish in life—we feel fulfilled and can help others as well. That doesn't mean there isn't a struggle, but it is one worth engaging in. It's said that the *daimon* bestows power—it is at once a source of inspiration and a silent guide—and becomes more accessible when we follow its creative promptings. In other words, the more we use our talents and act on our intuitive guidance, the more guidance we can receive.

When our creative spirit moves us, we seek companionship with a power more expansive than ourselves and intrinsic to our identities. We want to bring something that is essential to us personally into material form. And since we are a part of the natural world, our creativity is not separate from the creative powers of the universe; we all partake of one creative principle.

Each of us is unique, with our own personal history. Yet, at the same time, there is something about us that is more than our personal history. Although the things I write are informed by my experiences, emotions, family, ancestors, studies, worldview, and spiritual outlook, when I write, I meet a mysterious force that feels like something 'other' than myself and my story. What is this 'other?' Ancient spiritual traditions teach that you are a part of something greater but also uniquely 'you.' Only you can use and share the gifts you have been given, but you have the support of the *daimon.* Using the talents you were born with will help you develop creatively, evolve spiritually, and discover more about this "other," which is a more profound and expansive sense of who you are. When you follow your creative spirit, you make a stronger connection with the limitless potentiality of life.

Leaving a Mark

The artist wants to leave a mark, a trace. For example, when someone reads my words, some essence moves from what I've written to that reader's mind. One day, the magazine, book, or computer where the words live will no longer exist. But if what I've written leaves an impression, some essence will live on. This idea of a lasting essence also brings a responsibility to leave something of value.

You may agree with Anne Frank, whose account of her experiences hiding from the Nazis during World War II, *The Diary of a Young Girl*, has inspired people worldwide. She said: "I don't want to have lived in vain like most people. I want to be useful or bring enjoyment to all people, even those I've never met. I want to go on living even after my death!"[4] Frank lived her short life under constant threat of death and died in the Bergen-Belsen concentration camp when she was only 15 years old. Yet she attained a kind of immortality here on earth through her journal. Often, artists, those of us with a creative calling, are more acutely aware of the passage of time and our mortality. We want to leave something that will remain: a gift. There is no one way to create, and each of us must find our own path, continually overcoming obstacles that arise. Psychologist Rollo May expressed it aptly in the title of his book, *The Courage to Create.* We need persistence and courage as well as inspiration. I hope the methods provided here help deepen your connection with your creative spirit, stimulate insight, and commit to your art. It's a good idea to read the chapters in order, do the short writing prompts, and try the meditation practices. Then, go back and review what was helpful, disregard the rest, and incorporate what works for you.

You will want to have a journal, pen, or pencil (and perhaps colored pencils) to answer the prompts and to:

- Write your memories, inspirations, and plans.
- Record your dreams and the insights you receive from them.
- Draw your dream images and ideas.

Creativity is a habit, and the best creativity is the result of good work habits.—Twyla Tharp[5]

1. Acknowledge Your Daimon

At birth, every person is assigned a certain daimon, a guardian of life, to help with a destined task.—Marsilio Ficino[1]

During the Renaissance in Italy and other ancient cultures, philosophers spoke of interconnected levels of existence. They said that the level in which we live is the lowest one but that we can access higher levels; the *daimon* acts as an intermediary between the levels and can serve as a guide to help us use our talents and fulfill our life's purpose. Some traditions say we have more than one guiding spirit and that they come to us at different times, in different ways, and for various purposes.

Although in Greek philosophy, a *daimon* could be good or bad, we can consider a *daimon* that symbolizes one's creative gifts as a type of angel—a benevolent being—that comes to offer aid or assistance. The influence of the *daimon* can be seen in someone's natural talents and desires to accomplish some kind of life's work.

The Daimon's Challenge

The *daimon* bestows the gifts you are born to express, but it can, and usually does, present itself as a challenge. Any artist will tell you there is a struggle in creation, and you have probably experienced this yourself. Think of it as a mother giving birth.

The great Irish poet W. B. Yeats saw the *daimon* as a controlling power and felt that the poet needed to struggle with it to benefit from its gift of inspiration. "The *daemon* [embodies] all that least resembles the human, and [enforces] awareness of this opposition, through crises which shock the individual into recognition of its otherness."[2] The *daimon* is a part of you, but in a way, it can also feel as if it is outside of you, another being with whom you interact to create something new. It wants to awaken you to the truth of a deeper reality; through this awakening, you become a channel to bring forth a new form.

The *daimon* unsettles because, within the desire to create, you experience a compulsion, a drive that begs you to keep working. There will always be the desire to create more than may be possible because the *daimon* comes from an eternal, limitless dimension. The *daimon* urges you on, and you must find a way to let it guide you while modulating the energy so it doesn't overwhelm and dominate.

The *daimon's* energy may make you confront uncomfortable or challenging parts of your life. This discomfort is because your painful life experiences are fertile areas to explore in your creative work; they may be the compelling force behind your desire to create.

Although writing, composing, drawing, and all forms of artistic work can lower anxiety, help you come up with solutions to problems, and enable you to deal with the situations you face, you have to allow these feelings to come through in order to release them. There is a Japanese pottery-making technique called *kintsugi.* The artist fixes broken ceramics using a golden-colored lacquer filling, making the object look even more beautiful. When you work with our painful life experiences and create a work of art, a new form from your broken pieces, you also begin to heal.

The ancient Greeks felt that by using what they called *phantasia,* imagination, a person could hear messages from the divine source. In other traditions, imagination is said to endow the ability to get in touch with the unconscious and the dwelling place of the soul. When you use imagination in a disciplined way, you quiet the conscious mind and listen to what lies beneath. The imagination can be a bridge, a way to contact a deeper level of knowledge and wisdom. Using the imagination is how you contact your *daimon,* your creative spirit, and play your part in the greater whole.

Ancient philosophers said that the world's creation is a continual process and that we participate in it with our thoughts, words, and deeds. If you choose it, your task becomes to fulfill, at least in part, the potentiality of your talents, to try to bring your life in line with the intentions of the *daimon.* In this way, you also participate in this ongoing evolution. As written in the Introduction, *eudaimonia,* or flourishing, can be achieved when we have a good relationship with our *daimon,* our creative spirit.

Although fleeting, pleasurable experiences can make us temporarily happy, research has shown that taking the *eudaimonic* approach, seeking meaning and purpose in our lives, leads to greater psychological well-being and lowers the risks of

certain diseases. We become healthier in every sense
of the word.

Begin to think about persistent thoughts,
dreams, and urges. Years before I went to Italy for
the first time, I started dreaming of some Italian
words, and this was before I'd even begun studying
the language. I also saw mental images of a room in
Venice, a city where I went to live many years later.

Whatever your talents or desires, it's good to
keep a journal of your thoughts, dreams, and
feelings. Through writing, and perhaps drawing,
you can attain insights and find new perspectives to
clarify what you want to do. It's a way to organize
your thoughts and help you see the way forward.
Begin by answering the following questions in your
journal.

♦ Prompts

1. Have you ever felt something was
    encouraging you to move in a
    particular direction, study a subject,
    take a trip, or begin a project? What
    were you being inspired to do, or
    where did you wish to go?
2. Do particular ideas or images often
    come to mind? These may be
    geographical locations such as the
    mountains, the ocean, or a specific
    country or city. Or, they may have to
    do with a fascination with certain
    cultures, events, or people. Perhaps
    there are family connections, either

with people you know now or ancestors who have passed away, who still exert a strong influence. You might want to learn more about your family history.

3. In the past, when have you followed through on the persistent interest? What happened? If you did not follow through, what was the result?

Write freely without stopping for ten or twenty minutes. Then, read over what you wrote: did you learn anything that hadn't occurred to you before? Did you make any new connections about the things that intrigue you? These may become nourishment for your creative work.

2. Uncover
Your Personal Myth

The Greeks, a certain scholar has told me, considered that myths are the activities of the Daimons, ad that the Daimons shape our characters and our lives. I have often had the fancy that there is some one myth for every man, which, if we but knew it, would make us understand all he did and thought.
—W.B. Yeats[1]

What is a myth? And what does it have to do with the *daimon*, the creative spirit? In ancient Greece, myth meant a story or tale that held truth. A myth was said to reveal the deeper mysteries of life. Every culture has its myths, but as mythologist Joseph Campbell found, a common theme is a hero who must overcome challenging situations and confront difficult characters to attain their goal.

The psychologist Carl G. Jung also believed that every person's life experience has common archetypes or patterns. Many myths express similar themes concerning life events, such as falling in love, getting married, being trapped, hurt, or betrayed, and facing and overcoming complex challenges. There are also myths about cosmic events, such as the world's creation.

While we can study the great myths of various cultures to learn more about the forces driving humanity, we can also examine our own lives and discover that *each of us,* as the poet W.B. Yeats claims, *is living our own myth.* Each of us has a unique life story, with joys and challenging times.

When we look back at our lives, we can see patterns, circumstances, coincidences, or, if you prefer, synchronicities—personally meaningful coincidences—that have shaped our personal history. These episodes are the stepping-stones of your myth or life story. Looking at this story, you will find ideas that can color and shape your creative life.

Myth of Er

Although many people know reincarnation is a commonly accepted part of Hinduism and Buddhism, the belief is held among many diverse populations. Plato and other Western philosophers also wrote about it. In his "Myth of Er" from *The Republic*, Plato tells a story about choosing our destinies, and therefore our *daimons,* when we have finished one life and are about to begin another. This myth describes how, after death, Souls gather in the afterlife to choose portions of fate, or lots, as Plato calls them, that will guide them in their subsequent incarnations.[2] These portions of fate are like patterns we embody, akin to an astrological chart.

We enter this life, and we have a destiny to fulfill. But before we begin, we must pass through the plane of Lethe, forgetfulness, and so during life, we may not always remember what we are called to do. Yet our *daimon* does, and it uses various means to remind us of what that is when we forget or go astray. A Jewish legend claims the evidence that we may have forgotten our soul's purpose is embedded in our upper lip. This crevice is where an angel pressed its forefinger to seal the lips, and that is the place we often touch when trying to remember something. While in the myth, 'lot' means one's way of life or worldly fate, the word also means a small piece of land that can be used to build something or grow things. The more you act on your creative urges, the more roots you send into your 'lot' and the stronger your foundation for your work becomes. You are joining the greater power of Mother Earth, and mothers give birth to new creations.

Your Personal Myth

"What did you do as a child that created timelessness, that made you forget time? There lies the myth to live by." — Joseph Campbell[3]

When you explore your personal myth, you want to think of meaningful events in your life and see how they make a story that carries messages about what is important to you. You are the hero of your myth; you play the leading role. When you tell your story, you tell it in a way no one else can because only you understand how you felt; only you know what events or episodes were the most painful, the most joyful.

What are the moments in your life when you felt truly alive, when something seemed to 'grab' you emotionally, psychologically, or spiritually? Perhaps they are some of the things you wrote at the end of the first chapter concerning inner promptings, images, or desires. Woven together, they create a personal myth. Myths help us make meaning of our lives and point the way to our heart's calling. The idea is to develop an ongoing conversation with the meaning of your journey.

Lifeline

Create a 'lifeline' in your journal or on a large paper to record the trajectory of meaningful moments.

A lifeline, also called a timeline, can provide insights into your myth or life story. By creating and studying your lifeline, you can gain a new understanding of the significant events in your life, the effect they had on you, and how you might like to evolve in the future. Below is a spiral. if you prefer, you can draw your lifeline in a line or some other shape. The spiral works well because we often feel we are going through similar experiences as in the past. However, we are always learning and growing and can better deal with these challenges as time goes by.

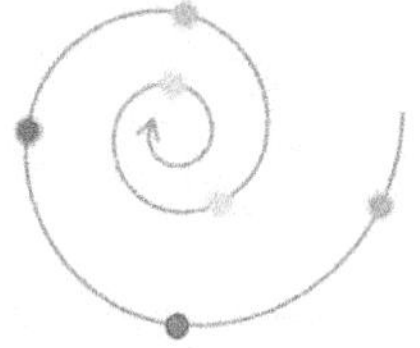

♦ Prompts:

Draw your lifeline, whether circular, straight, or some other shape. Leave room for writing on both sides of the line. Draw short lines to mark each decade of your life, past, present, and future. Write "Now" in the place that represents your current age. Start at the beginning of your life. (In the above image, your birth will be at the arrow point.) Write significant events from your birth to the present. Focus on when you:

- experienced significant growth.
- underwent a personal transformation.
- had a major life event, whether positive or negative.
- accomplished an important goal or couldn't meet the goal.
- were profoundly altered in other ways.

1. Choose an event and write what you experienced or learned.
2. Then, see if you can find a connection with one or more of the others. What do they have in common? Or how did one lead to the next?
3. What might your next significant event be?

3. Follow the Path of Love

Recognize the very few things in which something eternal endures that you can love, and something solitary in which you can gently share.—Rainer Maria Rilke[1]

Now that you have identified some critical moments in your life and the meaning they hold for you, think about the people, places, events, and activities you love or have loved. When we do what we love, we follow the *daimon's* promptings. When we love, we become inspired. The word inspired comes from the word spirit, from the Latin *spiritus,* meaning breath or the animating principle in living beings. Our breath keeps us alive, but in a more profound sense, *spiritus* or Spirit is what inspires and moves us to do what is important to us. A person's spirit is their very life force, and it bestows life, energy, power, enthusiasm, and will.

The Greeks believed that inspiration was given to humans by the gods and goddesses, who represented universal qualities and urges. Eros, the god of love, is one such force. And Eros is deeply connected with the *daimon.* In fact, love can be called a *daimon.*

In ancient Greek philosopher Plato's dialogue, *The Symposium,* the priestess Diotima tells Socrates that love is not a god but rather a "great daemon" and that "everything daemonic is between divine and mortal."[2] Ancient philosophers believed the soul was located around the heart area. Your

heart holds the image of your destiny and calls you
to follow it.

In a Greek creation myth, Eros, the god of
love, appeared out of a primordial state of chaos
and brought heaven and earth together, causing the
world's birth. To create, we need to open to the
chaos of our inner and outer lives, wrestle with it,
and refashion it.

Some ancient philosophers also said we live
in this universe with a particular birth image: The
exact moment when you were born, with its unique
arrangement of the stars and planets, had a special
quality that determines your talents and ambitions.
In the same way, we may think of the *daimon* as a
tendency or as a symbolic representation of an inner
and mysterious reality that calls you to do what you
deeply yearn to do, what you love. The Renaissance
philosopher Marsilio Ficino wrote that whatever we
love to do or want to try to do, what we dream
about doing or talk a lot about doing, has been
given us by the heavens or the stars—by everything
that came together to make us who we are.[3]

Love connects you with your fate, and it
concerns itself with your deepest desires. Falling in
love brings both joy and pain. You can fall in love
with a person, a place, or the idea of an artistic
creation you want to manifest. Although exploring
memories and past experiences for inspiration can
be difficult, engaging in these challenges, wrestling
with your chaos, and striving to make order in one
form or another brings your ultimate fulfillment and
enables you to find joy.

Mentors

It is essential to learn as much as possible about your given creative field and about others who have done the kind of work you want to do. Your creativity comes not only from your *daimon's* promptings but also from what you immerse yourself in and what you 'feed' on.

Creativity is about rearrangement or reconfiguration; you can find your place by connecting to those who came before. You become a link in an everlasting chain of creativity. When you become inspired by others, you will want to emulate them, not copy them, but follow in their footsteps and provide your interpretation of existing forms. After you have thought about the works and creators you love, the next step is to use them as mentors to guide you.

During the Renaissance (and even now), visual artists began by making copies of works they admired to learn techniques that could serve them in their work. Young, promising artists became apprentices with older, established artists to learn their craft. Only after years of study did the new artist develop their style.

As a boy, Michelangelo spent all his time drawing in secret. As his desire to learn more grew, his father agreed to place him as an apprentice with the great master, Domenico Ghirlandaio. Later, he studied ancient Roman statues that had recently been unearthed and used them as models for his work.

The father of the great painter Raphael was a painter and his first teacher. Later, Raphael studied with Pietro Perugino and painted works in Pietro's style. Leonardo da Vinci and other great artists also influenced him. Eventually, he developed his unique style.

The same idea holds for other art forms. For example, before mythologist Joseph Campbell began writing his books, he spent five years just reading. Choose works that stimulate you. Author Franz Kafka said: "I think we ought to read only the kind of books that wound or stab us. If the book we're reading doesn't wake us up with a blow to the head, what are we reading for?... A book must be the axe for the frozen sea within us. That is my belief."[4]

What kinds of books, music, dance, film, sculpture, painting, photography, or people wake you up and make you feel alive? What experiences stir, excite, stimulate, or make you laugh or cry, creating a sense of awe or wonder? You may find a particular writer, artist, musician, filmmaker, choreographer, or architect whose work you wish to emulate. This person can serve as an artistic mentor, whether living or dead. But there is a caveat: you can't follow anyone _too_ closely. If you do, you are not creating your unique path. To realize your potential, you need to follow your own unfolding path. Find mentors, learn from them, then integrate what you learn and discover your way. For example, choose one, two, or three people whose work you admire. Read about their lives, their work habits, and their specific styles. Listen, read, or watch some of their work

♦ Prompts:

1. When was the first time you remember doing something creative that brought you joy or that involved you in a way that you wanted to continue the activity, never growing tired of your work or play? What do you love to do? Where do you love to be? List things, people, places, activities, and ideas you love. Take one or more items on your list and write about the qualities that captivate or intrigue you.
2. Who are some people whose work you admire? What do you like about their work? How do they resonate with your creative impulses?
3. Record quotes or notes on aspects of these artists' work you would like to integrate into your work. If you are a painter, keep a file of images; if you are a musician, save a playlist.

4. Encounter Your Creative Spirit

When your Daemon is in charge, do not try to think consciously. drift, waiting, and obey.—Rudyard Kipling[1]

An encounter is an unexpected meeting, and there are inner encounters and outer encounters. Encounters that feel deeply meaningful in a personal way can inspire creative ideas. These encounters may be messages from your *daimon*, your creative spirit, prompting you to take action.

An inner encounter might make itself known as a yearning, a desire for some person, place, thing, or subject area. It could be a physical sensation, a dream image, or an emotion. Something is rising from the depths of your being into your conscious mind.

An outer encounter occurs in material form, for example, when you meet someone, visit a place, read a book, or hear music. Then, you may become inspired to want to know or learn more and get closer to the person, place, or experience. If you proceed, do research, put pen to paper or brush to canvas, and start working on a project, you may experience a third kind of encounter in which you feel a sense of *flow*, as if your work is taking place under the guidance or energy of some inexplicable force, that you are both steering and riding along with as a doer and a participant. Something feels right.

This wonderful feeling comes from the energy of your *daimon*. Over time, the more you focus on your chosen subject, the more you will want to maintain your focus. The longer you work, and as your project takes shape, the energy of your attention seems to create a magnetic field. It might feel like you have a partner, a friend, a companion—your project and you and your creative spirit are all joined together in a remarkable union.

When I begin to work, I have a rough notion of what I want to write about. I've gotten an idea, whether from a dream, a longing, an intuitive feeling, seeing something in the outside world, a book, a person, a film, a news event, or a combination of some of these. Something is stirred, and slowly, over time, the feeling grows, and an idea takes shape. Then I start to investigate more, read, research, visit a place, and take many notes. This back-and-forth interaction between the inner and outer worlds continues throughout the creative process.

At a certain point, I feel compelled to make a start. I'll begin writing, go back, do more research, revise, and plunge ahead again. When no more ideas come, if I lose focus or don't know how to proceed, I might start typing anything or writing by hand anything that comes to mind to get going again, to see some words on the page. Then I stop and read what I've written. Often, a phrase, sentence, or even a paragraph rings true. I start with those words, that sentence, and continue.

Flow

Any artist can tell you (and you may have experienced this yourself) that when they are involved in their craft, they enter a kind of altered state in which the intuitive sense kicks in, and they lose track of time. When you are in a state of flow, doing something you enjoy and are entirely focused on, you attain a state of unity. You become so immersed in your activity that it is almost as if you and your work are one being. And when you return from this state, you feel whole, complete, and at home in your mind and body. By entering a flow state, you can integrate the various parts of yourself.

When you do what you love and start to create, you generate energy, and the longer you work, the more that energy continues to grow. Renaissance philosopher Marsilio Ficino said that Eros, the god of love, pervades the act of creation. Whoever creates, loves.[2] And loving is a desire for unity with what one loves. Greater unity is the goal of the artistic path and the spiritual path. Renaissance philosophers believed that everything emanated from a divine source and that love, worship, and creativity came from a primary drive for fulfillment, to return to our source.

But love isn't enough. Creativity also takes the use of will. Eros, the love and desire to create, the source of inspiration, needs Logos or the ability to reason, plan, and execute. What's needed is the union of love and desire with intention and discipline.

Preparation

As written previously, inner and outer encounters stimulate our creativity, and the *daimon*, our creative spirit, connects us with what we find meaningful. The *daimon* may be considered a messenger from another level of existence to inspire and guide you. But what are these levels? Are they real places or imaginary ones? Aren't they deeper levels of your mind?

Whether the inspiration to create art comes from a mysterious place within or beyond you, you need to be able to tap into its source. Teachings from the great spiritual traditions have said that our true nature is limitless and eternal. The energy that animates you, the impetus that gives you the urge to create, the inspiration that allows creative thoughts to emerge—all stem from this true nature. Creation is ongoing, and we all participate in it, consciously or unconsciously, with our thoughts, beliefs, intentions, and actions.

How do you enter this dimension, this source of creative ideas? How do you begin to make order out of the chaos within and around you? Preparing your mind to receive is essential, enhancing your ability to focus and hear.

Listening

You may need to practice listening to the promptings of your source of inner guidance and test them out. At first, you may hear very little, or

various ideas may come into your mind. They may
not even be ideas; they may be feelings or hunches.
Sometimes, it takes a while to sort through what
action to take, if any. Some ideas may have to be
postponed, and some may take hold, and you will
want to explore them further, eventually
committing to a particular endeavor. There are also
times when you may have to remain in a state of
'not knowing,' just holding a question in mind or
staying receptive.

You can write, draw, take photos, and save
ideas in your journal, and doing so will create a
storehouse of impressions that you can call on time
and again. In keeping the journal, insights that will
act as a pathway on your creative journey may
come to you.

Creative breakthroughs can come in other
ways, after a period of intense concentration, for
example, when you've struggled to make progress
but have come to a block. A breakthrough can
happen when you are able to let go of whatever you
have been struggling with and turn your attention
elsewhere for a while.

The following famous story illustrates this
kind of occurrence. August Kekule von Stradonitz
(1829-1896)—known as Kekule—was a German
organic chemist. During the mid-19th century,
scientists tried to answer questions concerning how
building blocks created chemical compounds. One
of the compounds scientists wanted to understand
was benzene. Kekule had been working on this
problem for years, trying to learn how the molecules
in benzene were connected. He had several visions,
which eventually helped him solve the puzzle.

Once, he was sitting in front of a fire, and as he watched the embers flying up in circular patterns, half-asleep, he saw the sparks begin to look like snakes. Finally, the sparks formed a circle, like a snake biting its tail. This vision led him to come up with the structure of a benzene molecule in the form of a ring.[2]

Meditation

Creativity comes about through the encounter between seen and unseen forces in a zone that lies on the border of your conscious and unconscious minds. This zone is the land of the *daimon*. You need to remain receptive to the promptings that come from this space. They may be vague at first, and you may have to wait for the birth process to begin in its own time.

In our modern world, our attention is often pulled in different directions, scattered, and diffused by all the electronic devices and our busy lives. The power to accomplish a goal is only as strong as the attention you give to it. You must decide to focus and be able to stay focused.

Practicing meditation is one way to cultivate attention, patience, and active listening. Meditation trains the mind to stay on course, to return again and again to your goal no matter how often your mind gets pulled away. At the same time, meditation helps you let go of preconceived notions of how you will create and *allow* the creative process to occur instead of forcing something to happen.

By learning to rest the mind in pure awareness and become an observer of your thoughts, you grow more attuned to messages and signals, less caught up in 'shoulds' or 'shouldn'ts.' Creativity is a collaborative effort of your efforts and 'something else,' whether you call that the *daimon,* the creative spirit, your higher self, or your intuition.

A meditation practice can help you clear the inner obstacles preventing you from beginning or continuing a creative project. If a voice keeps telling you what you want to do is difficult or impossible, you will probably feel blocked when you start working. When you meditate, you let thoughts come and go without believing every one of them; in the same way, you can let your thoughts of not being good enough come and go, not dictate your behavior, and continue to follow your inner creative promptings.

We all have doubts about accomplishing what we want, and we may think we need more talent, time, or whatever it takes. Every creative endeavor is a risk; you never know if you will succeed. But meditation can help you detach from self-defeating thoughts. Creativity arises out of silence. In the same way that seeds grow from the dark soil, your creative ideas emerge from the deepest part of you.

There are various ways to meditate. One way is to focus on an external object, such as a flower, a small statue, or a candle. Another way is to focus on an internal process, such as the breath. You may keep your eyes open in a soft gaze if you are focusing on an object, or closed if you are focusing on the breath. You may also alternate between the two. Use mindfulness, bringing your attention to your moment-to-moment experience with openness and clarity, allowing thoughts to rise and dissipate without judging them as good or bad. Instead of following your thoughts, you become the observer of them or the witness. Whenever you find that you have followed a thought and become lost in it, bring your attention back to the object in front of you or to the breath. However, if you receive insightful thoughts about your creative work, you can remember to jot them down later. If you have not meditated before, start with a time frame that feels right for you. You may begin with five or ten minutes and eventually extend it to 20 or 30 minutes if possible. You may also engage in short meditation practices at different times during the day.

- <u>Clear a space.</u> Make the place where you meditate special in some way, where you feel comfortable and can relax.
- <u>Sit comfortably.</u> Keep your back upright, either sitting on a chair or cross-legged on a cushion on the floor. If you need to, you may lean your back against a wall. The idea is to find a comfortable yet stable position. You want to ground the body, bring your attention to your body's energy, and allow it to settle so that your mind can begin to clear.
- <u>Set your intention.</u> Before you start, resolve that you want to make the most of this time to be with yourself. Decide that if your

attention wanders, you will return it to your
'anchor,' the breath, or the object in front of
you.

- <u>Take three deep breaths</u>. Inhale fully
  through your nose, down into your body,
  and exhale fully. When you inhale, imagine
  bringing clean energy into your body,
  clearing away any blockages; when you
  exhale, imagine letting go of any worries,
  doubts, or fears have been on your mind.
  Then, allow your breath to take its natural
  rhythm.
- <u>Find a focus.</u> Be aware of your breathing
  without trying to control it. Pay attention to
  the space beneath your nostrils or your
  abdomen as it rises and falls. Your mind will
  wander into thought repeatedly, which is
  natural. This meditation is about noticing
  that the mind has wandered and returning it
  to your breathing or another anchor. No
  matter how often your mind wanders or gets
  lost in thought, return it to your point of
  focus.
- <u>Deal with discomfort.</u> If you feel discomfort,
  tension, tingling, itching, or stiffness, notice
  that, breathe into it, and try to remain in the
  same position or shift slightly. If you feel the
  need to move, go ahead and change your
  posture and then return to focusing on your
  breath or other focal point.
- <u>Dedicate your efforts</u>. Just as you began your
  meditation with an intention, end it with a

dedication. Make a wish that all may benefit as you have benefitted from this time.

- <u>Cultivate patience</u>. Developing a meditation practice is a life-long process. Over time, you will reap many benefits.

Some days, your mind will be flooded with thoughts, and other days, thoughts will come and go easily. Every day is different. If you feel disturbed by strong emotion, open your eyes and reconnect with your surroundings. Think of someone or something that makes you feel safe. Another kind of meditation is walking meditation. You can do this anywhere, anytime, indoors or outside. You can combine periods of sitting with mindful walking, noticing your feet on the ground, the movements of your body, or your breath.

Walking is also a great way to stimulate insights. Poet Wallace Stevens (1879-1955) worked in an insurance company and composed as he walked two miles to his office every day.

♦ Prompts:

1. Keep a journal by your side. If any creative ideas arise while meditating that you are afraid you will forget, write them briefly and return to meditating.
2. After you have finished meditating, expand on what you

wrote previously or add
additional ideas.
3.   If you are starting a project or
during one, jot down how your
idea will fit into the project so
you don't forget how it connects
to your plan.

5. Find Inspiration from Beauty

Every beauty which is seen here by persons of perception resembles more than anything **else** *that celestial source from which we all are come.*—Michelangelo[1]

During the Renaissance, artists wanted to create beauty to reflect the ideal beauty of the divine world. Philosophers said that by contemplating beauty and by making our world more beautiful, we could attempt to touch the higher realms.

Writer and philosopher Ralph Waldo Emerson (1803-1882) spoke of the beauty of nature and said that some, not content in admiring it, seek to embody it in new forms. "The creation of beauty is art."[2] But certainly, not all art is beautiful, and not all art is created out of seeing or experiencing beauty. However, even when, as is true in many cases, an artist creates out of painful life experiences, art can transform pain into a kind of beauty. We can feel moved and encouraged when we see a film or read a book in which painful events are told from a place of authentic feeling. The artist has transmuted their pain into art, and an alchemy of transformation takes place in both the artist and the viewer, allowing for recovery and growth.

What is beauty? We all know it when we see it or when we experience it. It seems from the first moment that we're born, we search for beauty, and we find it in our mother's and father's eyes, in smiles, and in all kinds of objects in the world around us.

Beauty is strong because it can transform our lives, yet weak because it can be forgotten or undervalued. For instance, our modern towns and cities are not always built with beauty in mind. In ancient times, beauty was valued as the prime component of architecture: "Beauty will derive from a graceful shape and the relationship of the whole to the parts, and of the parts among themselves and to the whole, because buildings must appear to be like complete and well-defined bodies, of which one member matches another and all the members are necessary for what is required,"[3] said Italian Renaissance architect Andrea Palladio. Beauty meant harmony, the proper relationships of elements, and grace; buildings also needed to blend with the existing architecture. Today, buildings are often constructed for commercial rather than aesthetic reasons, and many cities have lost their aesthetic harmony.

Although nature is beautiful, those who live in big, modern cities often must search for it.

When I returned to New York after living in Venice, Italy, for several years, I had to consciously look for beauty in green patches, parks, children's smiles, and small old buildings tucked between towering skyscrapers. Perceiving beauty helps us connect more deeply to the world around us and within us. And connecting with the world around us strengthens and inspires us. When we see beauty, we feel that the world is our home.

Many of us love art because we find it beautiful, but during the Renaissance, beauty was related to meaning. Renaissance artists strove to create both beauty and meaning in their work. By using the principles of harmony and balance, Renaissance artists believed they drew down spiritual influences when they created art. Leonardo da Vinci said, "Where the spirit does not work with the hand, there is no art."[4] When you create something that resonates with the spiritual forces in the universe and incorporates order and harmony, not only will you contribute something of value, but your work will truly come alive.

As you develop the desire to look for beauty, you may be able to find it in the humblest places and things. Photographer Diane Arbus found beauty in the uncommon and created photographs of those labeled circus 'freaks' and others who did not fit into the norm. Renaissance painters such as Leonardo and Ghirlandaio drew and painted the old and the deformed, and their works are filled with great beauty.

To deepen your familiarity with beauty and expand your ability to experience it in your everyday life, you should pay close attention to it when you experience it—take time to contemplate it and try to harmonize with it. Beauty may come as an unexpected gift; you never know when it will occur. One day, you are out walking, and the sun shines on a bush in a way that strikes you as exceptional or astonishing. The experience may have a poignant quality because you know it is fleeting and wish you could hold onto it, keep it from vanishing. Or you might be listening to music when suddenly the sounds take on a life of their own; nothing exists but you and the exquisite melody and notes. These experiences might evoke a sense of sadness as well as joy, and they take you by surprise.

Some might say they are like *visitations* from another realm, perhaps one of the higher realms the Renaissance philosophers spoke of. They have a numinous quality. Numinous comes from the Latin numen, meaning "a nod of the head" or "divine will." So numinous means divine, spiritual, or something given divine approval— a yes, an affirmation. Yes, you belong here; I see you, and you see me. We have met at this moment.

If you remain open to these kinds of unexpected occurrences and desire to create, you might feel a tension, an intense urge to do something with these evoked feelings. You yearn to transform your feelings into a work that conveys the meaning of your imagining. Record these beautiful memories in your journal. Describe what you experienced and what kind of effect it had on you. In this way, you become open to experiencing more moments of epiphany when something deeply stirs you. Noticing beauty gives you energy and life. Ficino said, "The world both lives and breathes, and it is possible for us to draw its spirit."[5] But it also works two ways. When you notice something, you give _it_ more life.

Seeing beauty and desiring to see it in many places, even looking for it, you also begin to feel more love. Beauty keeps you in the here and now, makes you come alive, and experience a greater connection to your surroundings. When you are in love with someone, the world takes on a new appearance. And when you experience beauty, you can touch that same experience of connection. You move from feeling love to wanting to share that love through the act of creation. Something is kindled within. Ficino, mentor to such artists as Michelangelo and Botticelli, said:

> …No one can ever discover or learn any art unless the pleasure of learning and the desire of discovering move him, and unless he who teaches loves his students, and the students thirst very eagerly for that learning. …whoever greatly loves both works of art and the people for whom they are made, executes works of art diligently and completes them exactly…artisans in all the arts seek and care for nothing else but love.[6]

Expanding your ability to find beauty helps you to perceive it in unlikely places and strengthen your tolerance for more difficult times and situations.

Meditation on Beauty

Using imagination, you can return to memories of beauty time and again. And by cultivating your imagination and memories of beauty, you will become ever more sensitive to new experiences of beauty. Contemplating these memories enables you to access more subtle realms of thoughts and feelings and open portals to the inner world.

Following is a meditation to remember and relive a moment of epiphany, one of those times when the beauty of a person, a place, or a thing made a deep, lasting impression. This kind of meditation comes naturally to us; we all do it when we daydream. Have your journal handy to jot down your feelings immediately after the meditation.

- <u>Sit</u> comfortably but upright with your back straight, either on a chair or on a cushion on the floor. If you need to, you may lean your back against a wall. The idea is to find a comfortable yet stable position.
- <u>Begin</u> by focusing on your breathing, then become aware of your body, wherever you are sitting, of the space surrounding you, and your feet on the floor beneath you.
- <u>Release</u> any effort to control the mind.
- <u>Let go</u> of attachment to the outcome.
- <u>Bring</u> your attention down and in, down from the forehead into the trunk of your body and interior. Attention to the body's interior is like sunshine and water for a plant. Everything that it touches grows. This energy you sense within you is sometimes called the "energy body," and it bridges your ordinary, solid, separate humanness and infinite awareness.
- <u>Recall</u> a moment of beauty, a time when you felt at one with what you were doing, when you felt fully alive and engaged.
- <u>Choose</u> to be in the feeling of the inner space of the revived memory: a particular place you love, with certain people, animals, or a special room. Immerse yourself in it and feel the love, peace, or joy you felt then.

- <u>Listen</u> and receive whatever message the feeling has or ask a question. Be open to what is communicated, whether a word, a feeling, or a sensation.

  ♦ Prompts:

    1. Describe what you heard, saw, sensed, felt.
    2. How might you use your experience as a starting point for something you want to create? If you are already working on a project, how might you incorporate the memory?
    3. Expand on the memory. Write as much as you can, providing as many details as possible, real or imaginary. You may not remember everything, but you might recall the feeling tone, and what it brings up in you now.

6. Make Sacred Space and Time

You must have a room, or a certain hour or so a day, where you don't know what was in the newspapers that morning, you don't know who your friends are, you don't know what you owe anybody, you don't know what anybody owes to you. This is a place where you can simply experience and bring forth what you are and what you might be. This is the place of creative incubation. At first, you may find that nothing happens there. But if you have a sacred place and use it, something eventually will happen. — Joseph Campbell[1]

The word "sacred" comes from the Latin *sacrum*, which refers to the gods or anything in their power, and from another Latin word, *sanctum*, set apart.

Just as a temple, mosque, or church is set apart for certain spiritual activities, it's good to have a sacred space where you do your creative work. Dedicate yourself fully to your activity during your sacred creative time, whether long or short.

If you don't have an area dedicated to your creative work, mark off a space temporarily, clearing away anything that doesn't have to do with the task. You might clear a portion of your desk, light a lamp, or place particular objects around you.

Ask yourself what your present purpose is. Decide to reach it and contemplate how to do it. Plunge in and keep going. Like anything, this takes practice and willpower.

Obstacles continually arise, whether through external interruptions or internal doubts and fears. Decide what time frame makes sense for you, then try to extend it. One way to increase the ability to use the will is this: When you feel you can't work any longer, try to continue for five or ten more minutes.

Rituals

Creating a ritual around the time and place of your creative work will notify your *daimon* that you are ready to collaborate and signify that you are making a commitment. Historically, rituals have been performed at the most important of life's moments, such as at rites of passage: being born, coming of age, graduating from school, getting married, dying—whenever a transition occurs, a threshold is crossed. A ritual is also often performed to mitigate negative forces and call upon the aid of positive ones. Religious practices use rituals incorporating certain words, gestures, and objects. Although communities often conduct rituals, you will perform your own personal ritual and can design it however you like.

Before I start to work, I clear a space on the surface where I work, and place only those papers and books pertaining to my current project. Sometimes, I listen to a particular type of music or read relevant passages from research.

There is no best way to work. Artists, writers, scientists, and other creative people famously have idiosyncratic methods. What works for one person does not work for another. There are many tales of the eccentric habits of artists, whether in their work or personal lives.

During the Renaissance, the number of artists grew, and their place in society rose. People studied their lives and habits. It was assumed that most artists were melancholy and lived unusual lives. Michelangelo neglected his appearance, lived alone, and was overly sensitive and difficult.[2] Leonardo da Vinci dressed extravagantly, kept to himself, avoided personal attachments, and was a perfectionist. Although he is one of the most famous artists of all time, most of his works remained unfinished.[3]

Some artists have regular writing, composing, or painting schedules, while others proceed more haphazardly. Composer Igor Stravinsky worked many hours daily, while writer Joseph Heller wrote his famous novel *Catch-22* in the evenings after working at an advertising agency.

No matter your situation, whether you hold down a full-time job or are free to create when you choose, you can find the time and the place. Toni Morrison (1931-2019) started writing by getting up at dawn while raising two children.

Schedules

Think about your daily life. What blocks of time can you carve out to do your creative work? There are no set rules for how long or how often to work. Yet, to accomplish anything, having some regularity is necessary.

I like to think of making a goal into a habit. Although holding an image of the outcome is good, regularly doing the work is even more important. Whenever possible, I write for two or more hours in the morning. Not only is this when I focus best, but doing what I love first primes my mind to concentrate on other, sometimes less desirable, daily activities. If you have a schedule with more limitations, here are some possibilities. You might:

- Wake up a half-hour earlier in the morning.
- Take time during lunch break.
- Spend an hour at night, after dinner.
- Block out a few hours on weekends.

♦ Prompts:

1. At the beginning of each week, create a work schedule. Choose a time when your focus is strong, and you know you can devote at least an hour (or however long you can and that you know you need to do your creative work). Decide which days work best for you.
2. At the end of each work period, write down what you accomplished and where you'd like to pick up next.
3. At the end of the week, summarize your progress.

7. Begin to Create

I am always doing what I can't do yet in order to learn how to do it. —Vincent van Gogh[1]

Once you have decided on your project, studied your craft, and found mentors, it is time to begin. You may never feel 'ready.' You may tell yourself and others that you're working on a creative project, but you might still be studying, researching, and preparing.

It will never be precisely the right time to start, and at a certain point, you must plunge in. Beginning any creative project is risky because you are moving into unknown territory, and you have to develop the ability to endure not knowing how things will turn out.

You're taking a chance because you must; something inside spurs you on. Making a bet to believe in yourself and your work can be both exhilarating and frightening, but this is the artist's life. The desire to create goes along with a need to go deep within, explore facets of yourself that require attention, and face what is both unfamiliar and what makes you truly 'you.'

So, while there is the desire to explore and bring forth what is within, there is also the fear that what you find may be insufficient or overpowering. But when you can use your will to act, to take those first steps, one thing will lead to another. You'll find that the more you work, the more ideas will come to you. You'll start interacting with your *daimon,* your creative spirit, and you'll feel a sense of fulfillment when you use your will and watch your project begin to take shape. The path may twist and turn, you may have many starts and stops along the way, and the end may seem elusive, but nothing can prevent you from arriving except for quitting. If you keep that place in mind and know where you want to go, you can continue moving forward.

Goals

Although doubts will always be there, setting a goal makes your dream a destination, and it helps you maintain faith that you will arrive.

Is your goal positive? When you achieve it, will you look back and say, this did me and others some good? Even if you feel your talents aren't strong enough, don't let that hold you back. Talent is only part of accomplishing something, and a lot has to do with persistence. But it's important to remember that the place you arrive when the project is complete will never be where you first imagined. Your vision will always exceed your execution, and you may never be completely satisfied.

However, no matter the result, you will have developed will, determination, and greater creativity for your next project and your life. While you work toward your goal, remember that every step may not lead directly to your final product.

If you're a writer, of course you'll have to write many drafts, perhaps go in a direction that ultimately doesn't make sense for your plot line and that you'll have to revise many times.

The more you work, the more you will want to persevere, and the more you will be able to perfect your craft. You'll make mistakes, and you'll keep on going. Eventually, you'll improve and grow in your ability to translate your thoughts and ideas into a finished product.

Belief

Belief is placing trust or confidence in a person, a thing, an idea, or something considered true. You need to believe in your ability to accomplish your goal to persevere until its completion. No matter what happens, if your work meets the approval of others or not, you will have succeeded. You will have learned and grown. What is success? Success can mean simply that you have made a commitment and are finding time and space to keep working on your vision, that you will see it through to the end.

Cultivate the feeling of success, whatever that means to you, and you will be drawn toward your goal, and your goal will be drawn toward you. You create out of imagination, so use your imagination now to experience the feeling of completing your goal. Develop the will to affirm that you can accomplish what you set out to do.

But cultivating this belief, this feeling of success does not come easily; it has to become a daily practice. You may want to create a representation of the finished project: a title, a book cover, a drawing, a description, an outline, or a symbol. And you must cultivate an intense desire to see it through because there may be moments when you feel like quitting. If what the ancients tell us is true, for each step you take, if you have a firm resolve, unseen forces will come to your aid. When you act on your hunches and intuition, the following steps will be revealed to you. There's an ancient saying: "The gods help those who are doing something." The more energy you put into your work, the more a corresponding vibration in your world will respond. When you can access and direct your creative energy, you are not only working toward creating a 'thing,' you are also developing your inner power. As you continue along your path and reveal more of who you truly are, you become a doorway for the divine source of creativity within you to emerge and find a form—the form you are in the process of creating.

♦ Prompts:

Create a SMART goal: make it specific, measurable, attainable, relevant, and time bound.

- Specific: Determine what you want to accomplish. This can be the complete work or a part of it, for example, a particular chapter or a rough draft. It's good to break down larger goals into smaller ones.
- Measurable: Identify how you will know when you have

achieved the ultimate goal or the smaller ones.

- <u>Attainable:</u> Believe this goal can be achieved. You may not be one hundred percent sure but choose to believe that it is possible.
- <u>Relevant:</u> Use your talents and align the goal with your purpose.
- <u>Time-bound:</u> Set a time frame in which you want to accomplish this goal.

1. Write your goal.
2. Write the date you'd like the project (or at least a first version) to be accomplished.
3. Then break down the goal into parts: what would you like to have done within three months? Six months? Nine months? Record these dates. Adjust your time frame as needed. But each time you make a change write the date when you would like the goal, or parts of the goal, completed.

Whatever you're meant to do, do it now.
The conditions are always impossible. —Doris Lessing[2]

8. Persevere

It does not matter how slowly you go as long as you do not stop.— Confucius[1]

Once you start a project, you need ways to keep going and move through the inevitable obstacles. Obstacles can emerge at the project's beginning, middle, or end. Initially, you may suffer from knowing that the road will be long, unsure, and hold challenges. Initially, you have a vision of what you want to create, but this vision will shift along the way. The product will never precisely match what you had in mind! Artists suffer from the difference between the vision and the imperfect realization of that vision. Still, you need to continue to reach toward the goal. And the act of reaching itself is a kind of fulfillment. You learn and grow by doing.

Some days will always be better than others. But there will come moments when you feel that you've dried up, that no new ideas come, that you are at a standstill. Then, you may need to take a pause. You might need to read something, do research, look at more paintings, listen to music, and fill your creative appetite with external sources. Or you might need to spend time in nature, be in solitude, enter the silence during meditation, and quietly wait for the *daimon* to whisper again.

Dream Work

Dreams have been a source of guidance since time immemorial; they have helped scientists, artists, and others find the answers they have been seeking. Often, symbolic, or informative dreams come after a period of intense work on a problem or a project.

A Russian chemist and inventor, Dmitri Mendeleev (1834-1907), reported the following dream. He had been "struggling to conceptualize a way to categorize the elements based upon their atomic weights. He later reported, 'I saw in a dream a table where all the elements fell into place as required. Awakening, I immediately wrote it down on a piece of paper. Only in one place did a correction later seem necessary.'"[2]

A dream can provide a symbol or the germ of an idea that might lead to any number of creative solutions. Once, I dreamed that a woman came into my room and wrote the word 'Venice' on the wall. When I awoke, I started planning a trip to Venice and wrote an essay on that trip that won an award from a literary journal.

If you feel stuck in the process of your creative work, try holding the question in mind before you go to sleep. Keep a journal near your bed, and record any thoughts, images, or dream stories you remember upon awakening. Then, write all the associations you have with the dream symbols. You might draw an image if it seems particularly compelling.

Over time, you may discover recurring images, patterns, or themes. By paying attention to dreams, you may find that they respond, providing insights that can help in different ways.

Swiss psychiatrist and psychotherapist C.G. Jung studied and interpreted thousands of his patients' dreams. He found that dream themes, characters, and images came and went, then returned, changed slowly, and revealed a pattern. He felt that people could see progress if they watched dreams over time. In the book *Man and His Symbols*, we read about the Naskapi Indians of Canada. The Naskapi speak of an 'inner companion' who 'dwells in the heart.' The inner companion reveals information through dreams. The Naskapi listen and test the truth of what is revealed to them and believe that the more they follow this guidance, the more dreams this inner companion will send. "Thus, the major obligation of an individual Naskapi is to follow the instructions given by the dreams and then to give permanent form to their contents in art."[3]

Focusing

Another way of gaining insight is by using a method called *focusing*. Focusing, developed by Gene Gendlin (1926-2017), a prominent American philosopher and psychologist, has been the subject of many studies at the University of Chicago and internationally.[4] Like mindfulness, focusing is an inherent human talent that can be cultivated. Focusing begins from the premise that the body contains an 'inner knowing,' which can provide more information about an issue than you might ordinarily be aware of.

Focusing consists of six steps: clearing a space, the felt sense, finding a handle, resonating with the handle and the felt sense, asking, and receiving. Focusing can be used to gain information on any problem or concern. In this case, focusing might help you find a starting or continuing point for a creative activity.

- <u>Clear a space.</u> Relax. Take a few deep breaths inside your body. Closing your eyes may be helpful, but you may also keep them open. Do what is most comfortable for you. Gently follow your breath down inside your body, noticing what is happening in your body right now without judgment. Bring a welcoming and friendly attitude to whatever you find.
- <u>Notice the felt sense.</u> Pick one problem. What do you notice in your body when you consider this issue?
- <u>Get a handle.</u> What is the quality of what you are feeling or sensing? Is there a word, a phrase, an image, a sound, or a movement that comes to mind?
- <u>Resonate.</u> Go back and forth between your felt sense and the

image or word that came to you. Does the felt sense and image seem to match? If they do, go back and forth to make sure.

- <u>Ask.</u> What is one small step I can take to express what I am sensing?
- <u>Receive.</u> Welcome what comes. You might get an idea about an action you can take on what you received.

You may not receive something specific each time you focus. But if you sense even a subtle shift, something has happened which will develop more fully over time. When you focus, you are looking for what is called a 'felt sense.' It may be vague, but the felt sense gives a general impression of a bodily reaction to a situation or a question. The shift or felt sense indicates that, by attending closely to the body's inner reality, something has changed, which can provide clues to the next possible step. But it's not necessary to have total clarity to move forward. The very nature of creativity is acting on ambiguous feelings. You are feeling your way forward.

♦ Prompts:

1. Write what you experienced during the focusing session. Did you feel a shift? Did an image, a word, or a memory come to mind? Although it might not

seem significant immediately, record it now and look back at it later or the next day.

2. Later, when you reflect on the shift, write what other details come to mind.

3. What's one small action you might take based on the shift? Write what you will do.

9. Commit to Your Art

I have sworn to myself to die painting.—Paul Cezanne[1]

When a situation requires a new way of looking at things, the acquisition of new techniques, or even new vocabularies, the old seem stereotyped and rigid…but when a situation requires a store of past knowledge, then the old find their advantage of the young. —Harvey Lehman[2]

We've all read about people who created famous works when they were quite young. Mary Shelley (1797-1851), the wife of English Romantic poet Percy Bysshe Shelley, wrote her novel *Frankenstein* at age 20. Helen Keller (1880-1968), who became deaf and blind after suffering an illness during infancy, published her autobiography at age 22. Mozart (1756-1791) started composing at five. Genius can be known early on, and accomplishment during youth is praised and rewarded. Undoubtedly, in certain professions, such as dance, youth is essential. But there are gifts of creativity at every stage of life.

It doesn't matter how old you are when you start creating. It may take you a lifetime to learn what you need to know and have the best conditions to do your creative work. For example, writer Frank McCourt (1930-2009) grew up in poverty, dropped out of school at 13, immigrated to New York, worked low-paying jobs, and joined the army. He later talked his way into New York University and became a teacher. He only started writing after he retired from a long teaching career, and his first book, *Angela's Ashes,* was published when he was 66. It won the Pulitzer Prize, among other awards, and was made into a film. He went on to write two more books.[3]

Author Harry Bernstein (1910-2011) published his first book, a memoir of his childhood in Britain called *The Invisible Wall* when he was 96—after 40 other books had been rejected. Only when his wife of seven decades died could he call upon his painful memories of growing up in Manchester, England, during World War I amid anti-Semitism and family trials. Bernstein won a Guggenheim Fellowship to pursue his writing and wrote three more books before his death at the age of 101.[4]

Whenever you begin, there is no way to know when you will produce your best work. Some artists experience early successes and subsequently go through a fallow period, or their subsequent works never measure up to their first. Others, such as Harry Bernstein, produce an enormous amount of work before finding their 'voice.' Some produce only one definitive work. Italian writer Alessandro Manzoni (1785-1873) completed his great novel *I Promessi Sposi (The Betrothed)* in 1823, but he continued to revise it for subsequent publications over 17 years. It is considered one of the masterpieces of world literature.[5]

In some cases, works of genius only become recognized after the artist's death. Between the ages of 27 and 37, Vincent Van Gogh (1853-1890) produced more than 2,000 artworks. But he sold just one painting during his lifetime, and he only became famous after his suicide in 1853.

Naturally, we all want our work to be recognized while we are alive! So much depends on when an artist lives, the culture they are part of, the hardships they face, and their life circumstances.

British writer Penelope Fitzgerald (1916-2000) was born into a literary family and attended the University of Oxford. Still, she spent much of her life struggling to raise her children and cope with an alcoholic husband. At times, the family lived in public housing. Fitzgerald didn't publish her first novel until she was 60, but she went on to become a lauded novelist, winning the prestigious Booker Prize for *Offshore* and the National Book Critics Circle Award for *The Blue Flower*.[6]

But you don't have to become famous or win awards to make your work worthwhile. Whether you are young or consider yourself old, the *daimon* lives within you and is your eternal companion, eager to see you develop your talent and bring your gift to the world.

Development

Pablo Picasso (1881-1973) was a child prodigy, painting when he was still a child. On the other hand, Paul Cezanne (1839-1906) had to work hard throughout his life to perfect his artistic skills. Some artists work quickly, others slowly. How long it takes to complete an individual work depends on many factors, including the individual and the kind of work it is. Graham Greene (1904-1991) wrote his book *The Confidential Agent* in only six weeks, although later he slowed down. At the opposite end of the spectrum, writer Donna Tartt took ten years to write her Pulitzer-prize award-winning novel *The Goldfinch*, which is over 700 pages long.

There is always the question of how to work, and each artist is unique. As E. L. Doctorow (1931-2015) famously said, "Writing is like driving at night in the fog. You can only see as far as your headlights, but you can make the whole trip that way."[7] You may be feeling your way through, and your style can evolve as you proceed. Also, you have to feel what you are creating in a palpable way. Poet Robert Frost (1874-1963) said: "No tears in the writer, no tears in the reader. No surprise for the writer, no surprise for the reader… "[8] He felt that a poem's meaning evolved as the writer discovered it in the writing process.

No matter your life situation and way of working, there will always be roadblocks that you think you'll never find the way around, and yet, with persistence, you can discover solutions along the way.

Doubt and Faith

If, as ancient philosophers taught, each of us is a microcosm or a reflection of the universe's macrocosm, then we have the energy that animates everything we can see, hear, touch, smell, or perceive within us. As astronomer Carl Sagan reminded us, we are made of 'star stuff,' and we consist of the same atoms formed in the stars.[9] Your *daimon* instilled in you the desire to participate in the world's ongoing creation, to contribute something of meaning and value that only you can do or make. Then, it's up to you to follow your intuition, tune into your imagination, and conceive of the form this 'something' will take. By cultivating faith in these principles and using the knowledge that you are indeed part of the universal whole, you can develop the will to believe in the value of your work.

You think through how you will accomplish your work. Then, you put your ideas into action, investing your feelings and experiences, both challenging and joyful, infusing the work with this energy.

When you begin your project, and even as you work on it, there may be a sense of separation between you and the work; you are initiating an action upon a material substance, whether the page, the canvas, the musical instrument, or the body. You may doubt that you can accomplish what you set out to do. If so, you will be in good company. Already well-advanced in his career, artist Claude Monet (1840-1926) wrote to a friend: "I'm never finished with my paintings; the further I get, the more I seek the impossible and the more powerless I feel."[10]

But as the work grows, as you craft it day by day, as you watch it develop, you will gain an ever-increasing sense of mastery, of knowing that you and the work are one, that you are expressing what is intrinsically a part of you. In this way, your sense of yourself will expand so that not only will your project take shape, but you will realize more fully who you really are—an inherent part of the divine plan and ongoing creation of the world.

Each of us has unique talents and ways of seeing the world, and in a strange dichotomy, while engaging in a creative act brings you into harmony with all beings, it makes you feel even more of an individual. You always seem to be moving toward becoming more expansive than before, in a continual state of transformation. In creating your work, you participate knowingly in the eternal process of 'becoming.' When you make a work of art, you yourself grow and flourish.

The creative process never ends. Prolific poet William Stafford (1914-1993) kept a daily journal for 50 years and wrote his last poem on the day he died. He said: "I keep following this sort of hidden river of my life, you know, whatever the topic or impulse which comes, I follow it along trustingly. And I don't have any sense of its coming to a kind of crescendo, or of its petering out either. It is just going steadily along."[11] He authored 67 books in his lifetime between the ages of 46 and 79.

His poem "The Way It Is" is a testament to the eternal creative process that can carry us throughout our lives.

There's a thread you follow. It goes among things that change. But it doesn't change. People wonder about what you are pursuing. You have to explain about the thread. But it is hard for others to see. While you hold it you can't get lost. Tragedies happen; people get hurt or die; and you suffer and get old. Nothing you do can stop time's unfolding. You don't ever let go of the thread.[12]

1. Look back at the lifeline you created in Chapter 2 on Personal Myth, in which you wrote about memorable experiences in your life. Where you left off, pick up the thread. Begin to mark off possible future developments. You might want to ask: What would I like to have created in a year? In two years? It doesn't matter how much or how little you have already done. Start from now. Don't let yourself be constrained by overly reasonable, practical thinking. This inquiry is not about definite commitments but what you would like to have. However, it helps to have a time frame.

2. Write a paragraph describing this future event, accomplishment, or creation.

3. Now, write the first step (and perhaps subsequent steps) you would need to take to make this idea come to life.

10. Share Your Work

It takes a lot of courage to show your dreams to someone else.
—— Erma Bombeck[1]

As long as you are in the process of creating a project, you can change, revise, and improve on it. Even after it feels completed and you look back at what you've done, there may always be more that you'd like to expand upon, edit, or re-do—and this process can continue indefinitely! As my college painting teacher, the late artist Richard Pousette-Dart, told me when I asked him how to know when a painting was finished: "What's the end result of your life?"

How <u>do</u> you know when you're done? The truth is you may never know. Yet, there comes a moment when it's time to stop and take the next courageous step of sharing your work with another person. Your creation must go out into the world.

It's essential not only to decide when the time is right to show your work but to whom—whether that is to a friend, colleague, or professional in your field. Until this point, you may have needed a certain amount of 'secrecy.' I have found that talking too much about what I am doing can drain my energy and open me to the influence of others who may not understand the nature of my work. As William Stafford wrote in his poem "The Way It Is," "People wonder about what you are pursuing. You have to explain about the thread. But it is hard for others to see."

As you progress, you may have several pieces of work in various stages of completion. At any given time, some of these works, your 'children,' may be strong enough to take their first steps, while others are still too fragile and need to be protected. When a fire is small, it must be kept from the wind. But when it is large, the wind can make the fire stronger.

It's a process of experimentation. Only you will know when to expose your work to others' eyes and ears. It's important not to do it too early, but you don't want to wait too long. And even after you've shown it, published it, or performed it, you may wish to continue revising. The first step may be having a trusted friend or support group, if you have one, provide feedback.

Getting Feedback

It can be challenging to take that first step and let go of your work, show it to others, and remain open to their comments while holding on to your belief that you've done your best; this process never gets easy. You will get some positive comments, and you will get critical ones. You may also get nondescript ones and think: "I poured my heart into this. Is that all you have to say?"

After showing your work to someone and listening to their thoughts and ideas, what next? Do you start changing, cutting, or revising? Do you agree with the suggestions they offer? Now, you need to take another step in both the creative process and your self-development. Reflect on their feedback, take a closer look at your work, and wait until you receive a clear indication of what feels right to you. It's your work, and only you can decide what needs to be changed—or left alone.

For writers, there are differing opinions on how much influence to allow when getting feedback. Some writers participate in workshops, showing their drafts to a group of people or several groups during various stages of the writing process and listening to everyone's opinions. This way of working may be useful for some, but it can be stifling and discouraging for others. Everyone will have ideas of how you can 'improve' your work. Some of these ideas may be helpful, and others could be harmful.

You might have one or more people you trust read your writing or view your art. Then, based on their comments and what resonates with you, you can revise or make changes. Finally, you could hire a professional and continue with the process. This process can repeat itself several times. However, if it's a short piece, for example, a story or essay, sometimes the only way to go is to send it to a magazine. If you receive a rejection, try to understand what made them say no. While one publisher may reject your work, another may accept it.

Whether a particular work is published, shown in a gallery, or performed in a concert hall, you must keep holding onto the thread. Although William Stafford wrote over 20,000 poems, only about 3,000 were published. Yet he maintained a daily writing practice.[2] Part of the creative life is developing a body of work over a lifetime. In this way, you enter a larger conversation. You become part of a movement, contributing to your development and the development of those who come after you.

Letting Go

If you've had the experience of getting excited about your work, believing it's worthy, knowing you've worked hard and long, and then receive rejection after rejection, it can be daunting to continue. Undoubtedly, the lives of many artists are filled with rejection.

Many famous and successful people have suffered setbacks. Before starting his renowned movie company, Walt Disney was fired from a job and suffered bankruptcy. Thomas Edison's teacher said she thought something was wrong with his brain, and his mother withdrew him from school to teach him at home. All in all, he only had three months of formal schooling, but as we all know, he went on to make many important discoveries and, in one instance, made 1,000 unsuccessful attempts to invent the light bulb—before he succeeded. Beethoven's teachers told him he would never succeed, yet he went on to compose some of the world's most famous symphonies, a few of which he wrote after becoming completely deaf. J.K. Rowling's *Harry Potter and the Sorcerer's Stone* was rejected 12 times before publication. And Alex Haley, author of *Roots*, wrote every day for eight years before finding success. Children's author Dr. Seuss, who wrote *The Cat in the Hat*, saw his first book rejected 27 times, while best-selling author Stephen King's *Carrie* was rejected 30 times.

Of course, these are the well-known "success after failure stories." But what about the rest of us? We need to ask ourselves: Why am I doing this work? Is it to become wealthy, well-known, or so that others will praise me? We all want to be recognized for our work, and we all need to make a living.

But the fulfillment you receive from doing the work must be the priority. The more you focus on that, the better your work will become, and the more determined you will be to continue. Just as you have to set goals, focus, create sacred space and time, and make creating a daily habit, you must train your mind to understand that it can take many 'no's to get to a 'yes' and that you need faith to believe that one day there will be a yes.

I know I will always write, whether all the 'yeses' I seek come. I do it because it's a way of life and my way of listening and responding to the prompts of my daimon. When I receive a no (and I have received many), I might fall into a depression, but eventually, I emerge and start writing again.

Here are some strategies to try:

- Use the 'no' to see where you can improve on your previous efforts. The timing may be off, and what isn't accepted now may be accepted later.
- Use the 'no' to see yourself advancing toward the 'yes.' One more 'no' brings you closer to 'yes.' Accept the

rejections gracefully and ask the person if they can offer you any comments so that you will understand what they didn't like. Sometimes, a 'no' means you haven't found the proper gallery, publisher, or school. Try another that may be better suited to you and your work.

♦ Continue to do what you love.

Baseball player Babe Ruth hit 714 home runs during his career. But he also had more than a thousand strikeouts. He said: "Every strike brings me closer to the next home run."[3]

Even if the yes doesn't arrive, you can say yes to yourself and find other ways to share your work. Create your own publishing company, find a space to show your artwork, or set up a shop online.

Art and Life

Once you've made your creative work an intrinsic part of your routine, your satisfaction from doing it can help with all your necessary occupations. You may find that you'll be better able to incorporate the principles of mindfulness, focus, and flow into everything you do, and your other activities will become more meaningful.

You'll probably have to do other work to support your creative pursuits. Accepting your current situation is the first step to manifesting a more desirable one. Struggle begets struggle, and acceptance begets more ease and flow, helping you move in your desired direction. Set your intention: for as long as you are doing the work you are doing, put in your best effort, and when it's possible and preferable to make a change, you will do that. Think of the values you want to incorporate into your life and work.

I did various jobs for many years while making what time I could 'on the side' for my creative projects. At one point, I worked for a wealthy man as his assistant. The hours were flexible, he was often away on business trips, and the pay was decent. I did have friendly co-workers, and I worked in a pleasant environment. However, the mission of the organization and the sense of leadership in a cause I could believe in were lacking. Also, although I was using some of my skills, they were not used for a purpose that I felt contributed meaningfully to society. A constant voice asked me, "What am I doing here?"

Early in my life, I studied to become a teacher. I worked in schools with students of various ages and abilities, and I enjoyed it. But I always felt that, eventually, I would leave teaching for something more personally fulfilling. I wanted a career in the arts—first acting, then writing. However, over the years, I realized that teaching fulfilled many creative and personal needs while benefitting others and that interacting with students and helping them reach their goals brought great satisfaction. Now, I have come to combine educating, writing, and coaching.

Even if changing your current job is impossible, you can change how you view your work and the services you perform. You can view almost any line of work in a way that emphasizes the benefit you provide to others. All your work can become part of your way of contributing to the ongoing creation of the world.

♦ Prompts:

1. From the following list, choose some verbs that you can use to create sentences that highlight the positive qualities of your current work or activities: Assist, Provide, Deepen, Implement, Help, Develop, Enhance, Maintain, Improve, Fulfill, Equip, Maximize, Deliver, Encourage, Entertain, Give, Inspire, Provide, Support.
2. Then, write a sentence using two or three of these verbs to describe what you do in positive terms. Perhaps you'll discover a way to use your positive qualities even in activities you don't find satisfying.
3. Now, write a sentence describing your creative work. Eventually, you can make all of your work align with your values.

For example, I can say that even in my assistant job, I supported my employer and helped him maximize his business. However, I realized I could use these skills to work more independently, make even better use of my skills, and help others succeed. Working with college students of diverse backgrounds, I find joy in their successes. I could say that I encourage them to deepen their knowledge, improve their skills, and live meaningful lives.

Enduring

Once you start seeing everything you do in the same light as your creative work, unknown possibilities may appear.

What you think upon grows. The more you do your creative work, the more creative your entire life will become. You'll find yourself applying the same methods you used to overcome obstacles while working on your project in other areas.

Whether you become a full-time artist or combine your creative pursuits with other occupations, the more you can bring your attention and positive focus to all your activities, the more you will have succeeded in living your purpose. If you're alive and in communion with your *daimon*, you are evolving. You are co-creating and contributing to the ongoing evolution of the world.

> *If you are born with a healthy mind, the stars will offer you some kind of appropriate career and lifestyle. So, if you would like the heavens to be kindly, you should take up this work and this way of life. Go after it passionately and the stars will bless your efforts.*[4]

Notes

Epigraph

- W.H. Murray, *The Scottish Himalayan Expedition* (London: The Temple Press, 1951), 6.

Introduction

1. Kurt Vonnegut, *A Man Without a Country* (New York: Random House, 1997), 24.
2. Stephen Mitchell, trans., *Bhagavad Gita* (New York: Three Rivers Press, 2000), 47.
3. Matthew Fox, Creativity: Where the Divine and the Human Meet (New York: Penguin, 2004), 5.
4. Anne Frank, trans., BM. Mooyaart, *The Diary of a Young Girl* (New York: Bantam House, 1993), 315.
5. Twyla Tharpe, *The Creative Habit: Learn it and use it for Life* (New York: Simon & Schuster,2006), 7.

Chapter One

1. Marsilio Ficino, De vita libri tres, Three Books on Life, A Critical Edition and Translation, ed. and trans. Carol V. Kaske and John R. Clark (Tempe Arizona).

2. Arizona Center for Medieval and
    Renaissance Studies in conjunction with
    The Renaissance Society of America, 2002),
    370. Julianne Davidow trans. This quote.
3. Neil Mann, "The Daimon,"
    www.yeatsvision.com/Daimon.html.

Chapter Two

1. W.B. Yeats, Essays and Introductions
    (London and New York: Macmillan, 1961),
    107.
2. Plato, Great Dialogues of Plato (New York
    and Scarborough Ontario: New American
    Library), 1956), 421.
3. Joseph Campbell, *Reflections on the Art of
    Living: A Joseph Campbell Companion,* ed. Diane
    K. Osbon (New York: HarperCollins
    Publishers, 1991), 148.

Chapter Three

1. Rainer Maria Rilke, *Letters to a Young Poet*
    (Mansfield Centre, CT: Martino Publishing,
    2011), 25.
2. Plato, *Plato's Symposium,* trans. Seth
    Bernardete (Millis, MA: Agora Publications,
    2003), 32.
3. Marsilio Ficino, *De vita libri tres, Three Books on
    Life,* 370.
4. FranzKafka, https://www.goodreads.com,
    https://tinyurl.com/ycysadzm.

Chapter Four

1. Rudyard Kipling, *Something of Myself and Others Autobiographical Writings*, ed. Thomas Pinnery (Cambridge, UK: Cambridge University Press, 1991), 123.
2. Famous Scientists. "Friedrich August Kekulé - Biography, Facts and Pictures," December 5, 2017. https://tinyurl.com/3fx55zm2.
3. Academy of American Poets. "The Wallace Stevens Walk." Poets.org, August 26, 2004. https://tinyurl.com/5b6vef4a.

Chapter Five

1. Michelangelo, "Paintings, Sculptures, Biography, https://tinyurl.com/4a7bxwdn.
2. Ralph Waldo Emerson. *Nature and Other Essays* (Mineola, New York: Dover Thrift Editions, 2009), 9.
3. Andrea Palladio, *The Four Books on Architecture*, trans. Robert Tavenor and Richard Shofield (Cambridge: MA: The MIT press, 2002), 7.
4. Leonardo da Vinci, "Quote DB," https://tinyurl.com/bde6btv9.
5. Marsilio Ficino, trans. Charles Boer, *Marsilio Ficino's Book of Life*, (Woodstock, Connecticut: Spring Publications, 1996), 96.
6. Marsilio Ficino, trans. Charles Boer, *Marsilio Ficino's Book of Life*.

Chapter Six

1. Joseph Campbell, *The Power of Myth with Bill Moyers*, ed. Betty Sue Flowers (New York: Doubleday, 1988), 115.
2. Rudolf and Margaret Wittkower, *Born Under Saturn: The Character and Conduct of Artists* (New York, W.W. Norton Company, Inc.,1963), 72-73.
3. Rudolf and Margaret Wittkover, *Born Under Saturn: The Character and Conduct of Artists*, 76-77.

Chapter Seven

1. Vincent Van Gogh, Quote Investigator, accessed June 24, 2023. https://tinyurl.com/5a2jwbye.
2. "Doris Lessing Quotes (Author of The Golden Notebook)," n.d. https://tinyurl.com/mr2pmhda.

Chapter Eight

1. "Confucius Quotes (Author of the Analects)," n.d., https://tinyurl.com/2p9k7k47
2. "How Mendeleev Created his Periodic Table in a Dream," *themarginalian*, https://tinyurl.com/yc75bjaz.
3. Carl G. Jung and M-L. Franz, Joseph L. Henderson, Jolande Jacobi, Aniela Jaffe,

Man and His Symbols (London: Aldus Books, Ltd., 1964), 162.

4. "What Is Focusing | International Focusing Institute," n.d. https://tinyurl.com/3yfrutuv.

Chapter Nine

1. Paul Cezanne, John Rewald, ed., *Letters* (Da Capo Press, 1995), 329-30.
2. Harvey Christian Lehman, *Age and Achievement* (Princeton Legacy Library, 2017), 330-331.
3. The Editors of Encyclopaedia Britannica. "Frank McCourt | Biography, Angela's Ashes, Books, & Facts." Encyclopedia Britannica, July 21, 2009. https://tinyurl.com/z8sr4z3k.
4. "Bernstein, Harry 1910– | Encyclopedia.Com," n.d. https://www.encyclopedia.com/arts/educational-magazines/bernstein-harry-1910.
5. The Editors of Encyclopedia Britannica. "Alessandro Manzoni | Italian Novelist, Poet & Patriot." Encyclopedia Britannica, July 20, 1998. https://tinyurl.com/mu598zs8
6. "Penelope Fitzgerald | British Novelist, Biographer & Short Story Writer." Encyclopedia Britannica, December 13, 2023. https://tinyurl.com/5d6uzu7p.

7. The Paris Review. "The Art of Fiction No. 94," February 24, 2020. https://tinyurl.com/tfmpda9r.

8. "Robert Frost Quotes (Author of The Poetry of Robert Frost)," n.d. https://tinyurl.com/3ytt47wp.

9. braincandy. "Carl Sagan - Profound Words of Wisdom," January 22, 2011. https://tinyurl.com/3dy8dkyp.

10. "20 Quotes from Claude Monet | Denver Art Museum," December 17, 2019. https://tinyurl.com/yc62k48e.

11. Bruce J. Wood, "William Stafford Poetry - Aoide." *Aoide* (blog), https://tinyurl.com/3v3mwhtu.

12. William Stafford, "The Way It Is" from *Ask Me: 100 Essential Poems.* Copyright © 1998 by William Stafford and the Estate of William Stafford. Reprinted with the permission of The Permissions Company, LLC on behalf of Graywolf Press, Minneapolis, Minnesota, graywolfpress.org.

Chapter Ten

1. "A Quote by Erma Bombeck," n.d. https://tinyurl.com/22zxyjfd.

2. Beloit College, https://tinyurl.com/ycku2p2u.

3. "Babe Ruth Quotes (Author of the Babe Ruth Story)," n.d. https://tinyurl.com/msxvbrmb.

4. Marsilio Ficino, *De Vita Libri Tres, Three Books on Life,* 370. Thomas Moore translated this quote.

Additional Selected Bibliography

Csikszentmihalyi, Mihaly. 2008. *Flow: The Psychology of Optimal Experience*. New York: Harper Collins.

Currey, Mason. 2015. *Daily Rituals: How Artists Work*. New York: Alfred A. Knopf.

Davidow, Julianne. 2010. *Outer Beauty, Inner Joy: Contemplating the Soul of the Renaissance*. Piermont, New Hampshire: Bunker Hill Publishing.

Galenson, David W. 2006. *Old Masters and Young Geniuses: The Two Life Cycles of Artistic Creativity*. Princeton, New Jersey: Princeton University Press.

Gendlin, Eugene T. Ph.D. 1978. *Focusing*. New York: Bantam Dell.

Harmon, Willis Ph.D., and Howard Rheingold. 1984. *Higher Creativity: Liberating the Unconscious for Breakthrough Insights*. Los Angeles: Jeremy P. Tarcher, Inc.

Hillman, James. 1996. *The Soul's Code: In Search of Character and Calling*. New York: Random House.

Johnson, Robert A. 1986. *Inner Work: Using Dreams and Active Imagination for Personal Growth*. New York: Harper Collins Publishers.

Kilung, Dza Rinpoche. 2015. *The Relaxed Mind: A Seven-Step Method for Deepening Meditation Practice*. Boulder: Shambala.

May, Rollo. 1975. *The Courage to Create*. New York: W. W. Norton & Company.

Moore, Thomas. 1992. *Care of the Soul: A Guide to Cultivating Depth and Sacredness in Everyday Life*. New York: Harper Collins.

Scruton, Roger. 2009. *Beauty*. New York: Oxford University Press Inc.

Stafford, William. 2014. *Ask Me: 100 Essential Poems*. Edited by Kim Stafford. Minneapolis, Minnesota: Graywolf Press.

Wangyal, Tenzin Rinpoche. 2022. *Spontaneous Creativity: Meditations for Manifesting Your Positive Qualities*. Carlsbad, CA: Hay House Inc.

Wittkower, Rudolf, and Margot Wittkower. 1969. *Born Under Saturn: The Character and Conduct of Artists: A Documented History from Antiquity to the French Revolution*. New York: W. W. Norton & Company, Inc.

Acknowledgments

I want to thank all the authors named in the bibliography and the people who have inspired me to listen to my daimon. They are my mentors in art and life.

Thanks to Cristina Lanza, Maria Liebhauser, and Bobbie Manning for your valuable suggestions.